ESE DUKE

What Our Church Leaders Never Told You

Unveiling the Truths Every Believer Needs to Hear

Copyright © 2025 by Ese Duke

All rights reserved. No part of this publication may be reproduced, stored or transmitted in any form or by any means, electronic, mechanical, photocopying, recording, scanning, or otherwise without written permission from the publisher. It is illegal to copy this book, post it to a website, or distribute it by any other means without permission.

First edition

This book was professionally typeset on Reedsy.
Find out more at reedsy.com

This book is lovingly dedicated to the Holy Spirit, whose guidance, wisdom, and power have inspired every word within these pages.
To the members of Spirit Temple Bible Church worldwide, whose faith and dedication to the gospel continue to be a light in this world.
To my beloved wife, Gladys Duke, whose unwavering love, support, and partnership in faith have been my anchor and joy.
And to all my children, who are my heritage and the living evidence of God's grace and favor in my life.

Contents

Acknowledgments	ii
Introduction	1
Chapter 1: The New Creation Reality	2
Chapter 2: The Finished Work of Christ	7
Chapter 3: Identity in Christ	13
Chapter 4: Authority of the Believer	18
Chapter 5: Grace That Empowers	23
Chapter 6: Walking in the Spirit	28
Chapter 7: The Power of the Word	33
Chapter 8: The Book of Life and Predestination	38
Chapter 9: Eternal Security and Assurance of Salvation	42
Chapter 10: Righteousness, Godliness, and Justification	45
Chapter 11: The Principles of Jesus and the Person of Jesus	51
Chapter 12: The Holy Spirit and the Church	56
Chapter 13: Loving Without Offense	60
Conclusion: Walking Boldly in Truth	63
About the Author	64
Also by Ese Duke	66

Acknowledgments

I give all honor and glory to the Father of our Lord Jesus Christ, whose boundless love and faithfulness have made this book possible. Without His grace, guidance, and truth, none of these words would carry life or power.

I extend heartfelt thanks to all those who contributed their time, prayers, and resources to bring this vision to life. Your generosity, encouragement, and belief in this work have been a source of strength and inspiration. May God richly bless each of you for your labor of love.

To the many hands and hearts that worked behind the scenes, ensuring that every detail was refined and every message aligned with God's purpose—thank you. Your dedication reflects the beauty of unity in the body of Christ.

This book is a testament to God's faithfulness and the power of community. Together, we have shared in the calling to reveal the truths of the gospel and proclaim the victory of Christ to a world in need.

Introduction

The Journey to Truth

In every generation, believers have sought a deeper understanding of their faith, yet many profound truths remain hidden or misunderstood. This book is not a criticism of those who came before us, but a call to rediscover the powerful realities of our identity in Christ, the finished work of the cross, and the unshakable love of God. It is a road map to the freedom, authority, and purpose that God has given to every believer.

Through the pages of this book, we will uncover what it truly means to be a new creation in Christ, to live empowered by His grace, and to walk in the fullness of the Spirit. These truths are not new—they are woven into the fabric of Scripture—but they are often obscured by tradition, legalism, or a lack of teaching.

This book was written to ignite a hunger for deeper fellowship with God and to equip you with the knowledge and confidence to live victoriously in Christ. It is a journey of uncovering what our church leaders might not have emphasized but what God has always intended for His children to know.

Together, let us embark on this journey of revelation, transformation, and empowerment, trusting that the Holy Spirit will illuminate these truths and lead us into a life of greater freedom, love, and purpose.

Chapter 1: The New Creation Reality

"If anyone is in Christ, the new creation has come: The old has gone, the new is here!" (2 Corinthians 5:17)

One of the most profound truths in the Bible is that when we accept Christ, we are made new; yet many believers still live as though they are bound by their old nature. Why? Because this foundational truth is often taught as a concept rather than a transformative reality.

What Does It Mean to Be a New Creation?

To be a new creation means that your identity is no longer defined by your past, your failures, or your circumstances. It means that:

- Your spirit has been reborn and is now aligned with God (John 3:3).
- You are no longer under the dominion of sin (Romans 6:14).
- You have the righteousness of God in Christ (2 Corinthians 5:21).
- You are seated with Christ in heavenly places (Ephesians 2:6).
- This reality is not a future hope but a present truth. When God sees you, He sees you in Christ—righteous, holy, and blameless.

The Old Has Gone, the New Is Here

When Paul says, "The old has gone," he is referring to the spiritual transformation that occurs at salvation. The "old" includes:

- Your sinful nature: It was crucified with Christ (Galatians 2:20).
- Your guilt and shame: They were removed by the blood of Jesus (Hebrews 9:14).
- Your former identity: You are no longer defined by who you were but by who you are in Christ.

The "new" includes:

- A new identity as a child of God (John 1:12).
- A new heart and spirit, as promised in Ezekiel 36:26.
- A new purpose: To live for God's glory and reflect His character.

Living from the Inside Out

Many believers focus on behavior modification instead of heart transformation. The truth is, that real change begins within. The Holy Spirit works in us, reshaping our thoughts, desires, and actions to align with our new nature (Philippians 2:13).

- **Renewing the Mind**: Transformation happens as we renew our minds with God's Word (Romans 12:2). This allows us to live out our new identity.
- **Walking in the Spirit**: Living from the inside out means relying on the Holy Spirit's power rather than our own efforts (Galatians 5:16).
- **Bearing Fruit**: The evidence of a transformed life is seen in the fruit of the Spirit—love, joy, peace, and more (Galatians 5:22–23).

Overcoming Old Patterns

Even though we are new creations, old habits and mindsets can try to resurface. Overcoming these requires:

1. **Faith in God's Truth**: Believe that you are who God says you are, not who the enemy or your past says you are.
2. **Intentional Choices**: Put off the old self and put on the new self (Ephesians 4:22–24).
3. **Community Support**: Surround yourself with believers who will encourage you to walk in your new identity (Hebrews 10:24–25).

Practical Applications

Declare Your New Identity:

- Speak what God says about you: "I am a new creation. I am righteous in Christ. I am free from sin."

Meditate on Scripture:

- Key verses: 2 Corinthians 5:17, Galatians 2:20, Romans 6:6.
- Let God's Word shape your thoughts and beliefs.

Live with Purpose:

- Recognize that as a new creation, your life is meant to reflect God's glory and lead others to Him.

Rely on the Holy Spirit:

- Ask the Spirit daily to guide you, empower you, and transform you from the inside out.

A Testimony of Transformation

Consider the Apostle Paul. Once a persecutor of Christians, his encounter with Christ transformed him into one of the greatest apostles. Paul's life illustrates the power of becoming a new creation and living out that reality.

Reflection Questions

1. Do you truly believe that you are a new creation in Christ? Why or why not?
2. What old patterns or mindsets do you need to let go of?
3. How can you intentionally live out your new identity this week?

By embracing and living in the reality of being a new creation, you can experience the fullness of God's transformative power and walk in victory every day.

> *"If anyone is in Christ, the new creation has come: The old has gone, the new is here!" (2 Corinthians 5:17)*

One of the most profound truths in the Bible is that when we accept Christ, we are made new; yet many believers still live as though they are bound by their old nature. Why? Because this foundational truth is often taught as a concept rather than a transformative reality.

What Does It Mean to Be a New Creation?

To be a new creation means that your identity is no longer defined by your past, your failures, or your circumstances. It means that:

- Your spirit has been reborn.
- You are no longer under the dominion of sin (Romans 6:14).
- You have the righteousness of God in Christ (2 Corinthians 5:21).

Living from the Inside Out

Many believers focus on behavior modification instead of heart transformation. The truth is, that real change begins within. The Holy Spirit works in us, reshaping our thoughts, desires, and actions to align with our new nature.

Chapter 2: The Finished Work of Christ

> "It is finished." (John 19:30)

When Jesus declared these words on the cross, He was announcing the completion of His mission to redeem humanity. These words encapsulate the power, finality, and sufficiency of His sacrifice. Yet, many believers live as though salvation is something they must earn or maintain through their efforts.

What Did Jesus Finish?

The Payment for Sin

- Sin separated humanity from God, and only a perfect sacrifice could bridge that gap. Jesus, as the sinless Lamb of God, offered Himself as that sacrifice.
- **Scripture Reference**: *"But He was pierced for our transgressions, He was crushed for our iniquities; the punishment that brought us peace was on Him, and by His wounds we are healed."* — Isaiah 53:5
- His sacrifice was sufficient to cover all sin—past, present, and future (Hebrews 10:14).

Victory Over Death and the Enemy

- Through His death and resurrection, Jesus broke the power of death and defeated Satan's hold on humanity.
- **Scripture Reference**: *"Since the children have flesh and blood, He too shared in their humanity so that by His death He might break the power of him who holds the power of death—that is, the devil."* — *Hebrews 2:14*

The Restoration of Relationship

- The tearing of the temple veil at the moment of His death symbolizes the removal of the barrier between God and humanity.
- **Scripture Reference**: *"The curtain of the temple was torn in two from top to bottom."* — *Matthew 27:51*
- We now have direct access to God through Christ (*Ephesians 2:18*).

The Implications of the Finished Work

The finished work of Christ is not just a theological concept; it is a reality that transforms how we live and relate to God.

Salvation is a Gift, Not a Reward

- Many struggle with the idea that salvation is entirely by grace. The finished work of Christ ensures that salvation is not based on our efforts but on His grace.
- **Scripture Reference**: *"For it is by grace you have been saved, through faith—and this is not from yourselves, it is the gift of God—not by works, so that no one can boast."* — *Ephesians 2:8–9*

No More Condemnation

- Because of Jesus' sacrifice, we are no longer under condemnation. We are

declared righteous in God's sight.
- **Scripture Reference**: *"Therefore, there is now no condemnation for those who are in Christ Jesus." — Romans 8:1*

Living in Victory

- The victory Jesus secured is not theoretical. It empowers us to overcome sin, fear, and the enemy.
- **Scripture Reference**: *"But thanks be to God! He gives us the victory through our Lord Jesus Christ." — 1 Corinthians 15:57*

Living in the Reality of His Work

Understanding the finished work of Christ empowers us to:

Rest in His Love

- Stop striving for approval. God's love is unconditional, and His acceptance is based on what Jesus accomplished.
- **Practical Application**: Spend time in worship, thanking God for His grace and love.

Approach God with Boldness

- The finished work gives us confidence to come before God in prayer and worship without fear.
- **Scripture Reference**: *"Let us then approach God's throne of grace with confidence, so that we may receive mercy and find grace to help us in our time of need." — Hebrews 4:16*

Walk in Freedom

- We are no longer slaves to sin. The power of sin has been broken, and we

can live in freedom.
- **Scripture Reference**: *"For sin shall no longer be your master, because you are not under the law, but under grace."* — Romans 6:14

Challenges to Embracing the Finished Work

Legalism

- Some believers fall into the trap of trying to earn God's favor through rules and rituals, forgetting that Jesus already fulfilled the law on their behalf.

Condemnation and Guilt

- The enemy often uses guilt to make us doubt the sufficiency of Jesus' work. But the blood of Jesus cleanses us from all unrighteousness (1 John 1:9).

Unbelief

- Fully embracing the finished work requires faith. Doubt can keep us from experiencing the fullness of God's promises.

Practical Applications

Meditate on the Cross

- Reflect on what Jesus accomplished for you. Consider passages like Isaiah 53, John 19, and Hebrews 10.

Celebrate Communion

- Holy Communion is a reminder of the finished work of Christ. Approach it with gratitude and reverence.

Share the Gospel

- The message of the finished work is the heart of the gospel. Share it boldly with others.

Reflection Questions

1. How does understanding the finished work of Christ change the way you approach God?
2. Are there areas in your life where you still feel the need to strive for approval? How can you rest in His grace?
3. What steps can you take to live more fully in the victory Jesus secured for you?

By embracing the finished work of Christ, we can experience the fullness of salvation, live in victory, and walk in the confidence that we are deeply loved and fully accepted by God.

"It is finished." —John 19:30

When Jesus declared these words on the cross, He was announcing the completion of His mission to redeem humanity. Yet, many believers live as though salvation is something they must earn or maintain through their efforts.

What Did Jesus Finish?

- **The payment for sin**: Jesus' sacrifice was sufficient to cover all sin—past, present, and future (Hebrews 10:14).
- **Victory over death and the enemy**: Through His resurrection, Jesus triumphed over the power of the grave and Satan (Colossians 2:15).
- **The restoration of relationship**: The veil in the temple was torn, symbolizing that we now have direct access to God (Matthew 27:51).

Living in the Reality of His Work

Understanding the finished work of Christ empowers us to:

- Stop striving for approval and rest in God's love.
- Approach God with boldness and confidence (Hebrews 4:16).
- Walk in victory over sin and condemnation (Romans 8:1).

Chapter 3: Identity in Christ

"As He is, so are we in this world." (1 John 4:17)

Understanding our identity in Christ is foundational to living the victorious Christian life. Yet, many believers struggle to fully grasp who they are in Christ, often living far below the spiritual inheritance God has provided.

Who You Are in Christ

When you are born again, your identity is completely transformed. You are:

A Child of God

- You are no longer a slave to sin but a beloved child of the Father.
- **Scripture Reference**: *"See what great love the Father has lavished on us, that we should be called children of God! And that is what we are!"* — 1 John 3:1

An Heir of God's Promises

- As children of God, we are heirs to all His promises.
- **Scripture Reference**: *"Now if we are children, then we are heirs—heirs of God and co-heirs with Christ."* — Romans 8:17

A New Creation

- Your old identity is gone; you are a new creation in Christ.
- **Scripture Reference**: *"Therefore, if anyone is in Christ, the new creation has come: The old has gone, the new is here!"* — 2 Corinthians 5:17

Righteous in Christ

- Righteousness is not something we earn; it is a gift given through Christ.
- **Scripture Reference**: *"God made Him who had no sin to be sin for us, so that in Him we might become the righteousness of God."* — 2 Corinthians 5:21

Overcoming Identity Crises

Many believers struggle with feelings of inadequacy, guilt, or unworthiness. These feelings stem from a lack of understanding of our new identity in Christ. By embracing our identity, we can:

Silence the Lies of the Enemy

- The enemy's primary strategy is deception. He wants us to doubt our worth and our place in God's kingdom.
- **Practical Application**: Combat the lies of the enemy with the truth of Scripture. Speak God's Word over your life.

Live with Purpose and Confidence

- Knowing who you are in Christ allows you to walk boldly in your calling.
- **Illustration**: A prince or princess behaves differently because they understand their royal status. Likewise, we should live in alignment with our identity as heirs of God's kingdom.

Reflect God's Glory

- As God's children, we are called to reflect His character and love to the world.
- **Scripture Reference**: *"Let your light shine before others, that they may see your good deeds and glorify your Father in heaven."* — Matthew 5:16

Practical Steps to Embrace Your Identity

Meditate on God's Word

- Immerse yourself in Scriptures that affirm your identity in Christ, such as Ephesians 1 and Romans 8.

Renew Your Mind

- Transformation begins with the renewal of your mind. Replace negative thoughts with the truth of God's Word.
- **Scripture Reference**: *"Do not conform to the pattern of this world, but be transformed by the renewing of your mind."* — Romans 12:2

Walk in the Spirit

- Rely on the Holy Spirit to guide, empower, and affirm your identity in Christ.
- **Scripture Reference**: *"The Spirit Himself testifies with our spirit that we are God's children."* — Romans 8:16

Speak Life Over Yourself

- Declare who you are in Christ. Say things like, "I am loved," "I am righteous," "I am victorious."

- **Illustration**: A child who hears affirmations of love and value grows in confidence. As God's children, we need to hear and speak His affirmations over ourselves.

The Role of Faith in Identity

Believing in your identity in Christ requires faith. It's not about feelings but about standing on the truth of God's Word.

- **Scripture Reference**: *"And without faith it is impossible to please God, because anyone who comes to Him must believe that He exists and that He rewards those who earnestly seek Him."* — Hebrews 11:6

Faith activates the reality of our identity, allowing us to live in the fullness of who God says we are.

Reflection Questions

1. Do you see yourself as God sees you? If not, what steps can you take to align your perspective with His?
2. What lies have you believed about your identity, and how can you replace them with the truth?
3. How can you reflect your identity in Christ in your daily interactions?

By understanding and embracing our identity in Christ, we can live with purpose, confidence, and boldness, reflecting God's glory in every area of our lives.

> *"As He is, so are we in this world."* (1 John 4:17)

Our identity as believers is not something we create; it is something we receive. In Christ, we are:

- Sons and daughters of God (Galatians 4:6–7).
- Heirs of His promises (Romans 8:17).
- Ambassadors of His kingdom (2 Corinthians 5:20).

Overcoming Identity Crises

Many believers struggle with feelings of inadequacy, guilt, or unworthiness. These struggles stem from a misunderstanding of who we are in Christ. By embracing our identity, we can:

- Silence the lies of the enemy.
- Live with purpose and confidence.
- Reflect God's glory in every area of our lives.

Chapter 4: Authority of the Believer

"I have given you authority to trample on snakes and scorpions and to overcome all the power of the enemy." (Luke 10:19)

Authority is one of the most misunderstood aspects of the believer's life. Many Christians live in fear, unaware that they have been given power over the enemy through Christ. This authority is not a result of our own merit but is rooted in our identity as children of God and the finished work of Christ.

Understanding Our Authority

Authority Through Christ

- Jesus secured authority over all powers and principalities through His death and resurrection.
- **Scripture Reference**: *"And having disarmed the powers and authorities, He made a public spectacle of them, triumphing over them by the cross."* — Colossians 2:15

Seated with Christ

- As believers, we are spiritually seated with Christ in heavenly places, sharing in His authority.

- **Scripture Reference**: *"And God raised us up with Christ and seated us with Him in the heavenly realms in Christ Jesus."* — Ephesians 2:6

Delegated Authority

- Jesus has given us His authority to enforce His victory on earth.
- **Scripture Reference**: *"Truly I tell you, whatever you bind on earth will be bound in heaven, and whatever you loose on earth will be loosed in heaven."* — Matthew 18:18

Walking in Authority

Understanding Your Position

- Authority flows from identity. You must know who you are in Christ to exercise spiritual authority effectively.
- **Illustration**: A police officer's authority is not in their physical strength but in their position and the power backing them. Similarly, our authority is backed by the power of heaven.

Using Your Words

- Life and death are in the power of the tongue. When we speak God's Word, we release His power into situations.
- **Scripture Reference**: *"The tongue has the power of life and death, and those who love it will eat its fruit."* — Proverbs 18:21
- **Practical Application**: Speak declarations over your life, family, and situations, aligning your words with God's promises.

Resisting the Enemy

- Submission to God and active resistance against the enemy cause him to flee.

- **Scripture Reference**: *"Submit yourselves, then, to God. Resist the devil, and he will flee from you."* — *James 4:7*

Enemies of Spiritual Authority

Ignorance

- Many believers are unaware of their authority, living in defeat and fear.
- **Scripture Reference**: *"My people are destroyed for lack of knowledge."* — *Hosea 4:6*

Unbelief

- Doubting God's Word and promises hinders the exercise of authority.
- **Illustration**: Peter walked on water until he doubted. Faith is essential to walking in authority.

Disobedience

- Sin and disobedience weaken our ability to walk confidently in our authority.
- **Scripture Reference**: *"If I had cherished sin in my heart, the Lord would not have listened."* — *Psalm 66:18*

Practical Applications

Daily Submission to God

- Authority begins with surrendering to God's will and aligning with His purposes.
- **Scripture Reference**: *"Trust in the Lord with all your heart and lean not on your own understanding; in all your ways submit to Him, and He will make your paths straight."* — *Proverbs 3:5–6*

CHAPTER 4: AUTHORITY OF THE BELIEVER

Declare God's Promises

- Speak Scripture over your life and circumstances. For example:
- "I have the mind of Christ" (*1 Corinthians 2:16*).
- "No weapon formed against me shall prosper" (*Isaiah 54:17*).

Stand Firm in Faith

- Faith activates authority. Believe that what you declare in alignment with God's Word will come to pass.
- **Scripture Reference**: *"Therefore I tell you, whatever you ask for in prayer, believe that you have received it, and it will be yours."* — Mark 11:24

Engage in Prayer and Intercession

- Prayer is the battlefield where spiritual authority is exercised.
- **Scripture Reference**: *"The prayer of a righteous person is powerful and effective."* — James 5:16

Reflection Questions

1. Do you understand the authority you have as a believer in Christ? If not, what steps can you take to learn more?
2. Are there areas in your life where you are not exercising authority? How can you begin to take a stand?
3. How can you align your words and actions with the authority God has given you?

Empowering Declarations

- I am seated with Christ in heavenly places.
- I have authority over all the power of the enemy.
- No weapon formed against me shall prosper.

- I submit to God and resist the enemy, and he must flee.
- I declare that God's promises for my life will come to pass.

By understanding and walking in the authority God has given us, we can live boldly, overcome challenges, and fulfill our divine purpose on earth.

> *"I have given you authority to trample on snakes and scorpions and to overcome all the power of the enemy." (Luke 10:19)*

Authority is one of the most misunderstood aspects of the believer's life. Many Christians live in fear, unaware that they have been given power over the enemy through Christ.

Walking in Authority

- **Understanding your position**: As believers, we are seated with Christ in heavenly places (Ephesians 2:6).
- **Using your words**: Life and death are in the power of the tongue (Proverbs 18:21). We are called to speak God's Word with authority.
- **Resisting the enemy**: Submission to God and resistance to the devil cause him to flee (James 4:7).

Chapter 5: Grace That Empowers

"For it is by grace you have been saved, through faith—and this is not from yourselves, it is the gift of God." (Ephesians 2:8)

Grace is often misunderstood as mere leniency toward sin. However, grace is much more than forgiveness. It is the empowering presence of God that enables us to live victoriously and fulfill His purposes for our lives. Grace is at the heart of the gospel, revealing God's unmerited favor and His transformative power.

What Is Grace?

Grace is:

Unmerited Favor:

- It is God's gift to us. It is given not because we deserve it but because He loves us.
- **Scripture Reference**: *"But God demonstrates His own love for us in this: While we were still sinners, Christ died for us."* — Romans 5:8

Empowerment for Godly Living:

- Grace does not merely save us; it empowers us to live a life that reflects

God's character and glory.
- **Scripture Reference**: *"For the grace of God has appeared that offers salvation to all people. It teaches us to say 'No' to ungodliness and worldly passions, and to live self-controlled, upright and godly lives in this present age."* — Titus 2:11–12

The Foundation of Our Relationship with God:

- Grace brings us into relationship with God, sustaining us and enabling us to grow in Him.
- **Scripture Reference**: *"Let us then approach God's throne of grace with confidence, so that we may receive mercy and find grace to help us in our time of need."* — Hebrews 4:16

Grace and the Finished Work of Christ

The grace we receive is rooted in the finished work of Christ. At the cross:

- Jesus paid the penalty for sin opening the way for us to receive God's grace freely.
- He fulfilled the law, ensuring that grace replaces legalism as the basis of our relationship with God.
- Grace empowers us to live in victory, not by our own efforts but through His Spirit.

The Empowering Nature of Grace

Grace Transforms Lives:

- Grace doesn't leave us where we are; it changes us from the inside out.
- **Scripture Reference**: *"Do not be conformed to the pattern of this world, but be transformed by the renewing of your mind."* — Romans 12:2

Grace Enables Holiness:

- Grace is not a license to sin but the power to overcome it.
- **Scripture Reference**: *"What then? Shall we sin because we are not under the law but under grace? By no means!"* — Romans 6:15

Grace Gives Us Strength:

- In moments of weakness, grace sustains and strengthens us.
- **Scripture Reference**: *"My grace is sufficient for you, for My power is made perfect in weakness."* — 2 Corinthians 12:9

Living in the Power of Grace

Receive Grace by Faith:

- Grace is available to all, but it must be received through faith.
- **Scripture Reference**: *"For it is by grace you have been saved, through faith—and this is not from yourselves, it is the gift of God."* — Ephesians 2:8

Grow in Grace:

- Grace is not static; we are called to grow in our understanding and application of it.
- **Scripture Reference**: *"But grow in the grace and knowledge of our Lord and Savior Jesus Christ. To Him be glory both now and forever! Amen."* — 2 Peter 3:18

Extend Grace to Others:

- As recipients of God's grace, we are called to show grace to others.
- **Scripture Reference**: *"Be kind and compassionate to one another, forgiving each other, just as in Christ God forgave you."* — Ephesians 4:32

Practical Applications

Live Dependently on God:

- Rely on His grace daily for strength, wisdom, and guidance.

Reflect Grace in Relationships:

- Be quick to forgive, patient with others, and generous in your actions.

Declare the Truth of Grace:

- Speak the promises of grace over your life, affirming that you are empowered by God's Spirit.

Common Misunderstandings About Grace

Grace as a License to Sin:

- Grace empowers us to live righteously, not to indulge in sin.

Earning Grace:

- Grace is a gift, not something we can earn through good works.
- **Scripture Reference:** *"And if by grace, then it cannot be based on works; if it were, grace would no longer be grace."* — Romans 11:6

Grace as Weakness:

- Grace is not passive but powerful, enabling us to live boldly for God.

Reflection Questions

1. How has God's grace transformed your life?
2. Are there areas where you need to rely more on His grace?
3. How can you extend grace to those around you?

Empowering Declarations

- I live by the grace of God, which empowers me to walk in victory.
- God's grace is sufficient for every area of my life.
- Through grace, I overcome sin and live righteously.
- I extend the grace I have received to others, reflecting God's love.
- I grow daily in the grace and knowledge of Jesus Christ.

By embracing the fullness of God's grace, we can live victoriously, reflecting His love and glory in every area of our lives.

> *"For it is by grace you have been saved, through faith—and this is not from yourselves, it is the gift of God." (Ephesians 2:8)*

Grace is often misunderstood as mere leniency toward sin. However, grace is much more than forgiveness. It is the empowering presence of God that enables us to live victoriously.

The Empowering Nature of Grace

- Grace teaches us to say no to ungodliness (Titus 2:11–12).
- Grace equips us to serve God effectively (1 Corinthians 15:10).
- Grace gives us access to God's strength in our weakness (2 Corinthians 12:9).

Chapter 6: Walking in the Spirit

"Since we live by the Spirit, let us keep in step with the Spirit."
(Galatians 5:25)

Walking in the Spirit is essential for living the victorious Christian life. It is not a passive process but an active and intentional pursuit of God's will and presence in every area of our lives. When we walk in the Spirit, we align ourselves with His leading, allowing Him to empower and transform us from within.

What Does It Mean to Walk in the Spirit?

Living in Dependence on the Holy Spirit:

- Walking in the Spirit means relying on the Holy Spirit for guidance, strength, and wisdom in all things.
- **Scripture Reference**: *"Trust in the Lord with all your heart and lean not on your own understanding; in all your ways submit to Him, and He will make your paths straight."* — Proverbs 3:5–6

Aligning with God's Word:

- The Spirit and the Word of God work in harmony. Walking in the Spirit requires meditating on and obeying God's Word.

- **Scripture Reference**: *"Your word is a lamp to my feet and a light for my path."* — Psalm 119:105

Bearing the Fruit of the Spirit:

- The evidence of walking in the Spirit is the fruit that it produces in our lives—love, joy, peace, patience, kindness, goodness, faithfulness, gentleness, and self-control.
- **Scripture Reference**: *"But the fruit of the Spirit is love, joy, peace, forbearance, kindness, goodness, faithfulness, gentleness and self-control."* — Galatians 5:22–23

The Benefits of Walking in the Spirit

Victory Over the Flesh:

- The flesh represents our sinful nature and desires. Walking in the Spirit empowers us to overcome temptation and live righteously.
- **Scripture Reference**: *"So I say, walk by the Spirit, and you will not gratify the desires of the flesh."* — Galatians 5:16

Clarity and Guidance:

- The Holy Spirit directs our steps, ensuring we remain on God's path for our lives.
- **Scripture Reference**: *"Whether you turn to the right or to the left, your ears will hear a voice behind you, saying, 'This is the way; walk in it.'"* — Isaiah 30:21

Empowerment for Ministry:

- Walking in the Spirit equips us with spiritual gifts and boldness to fulfill God's purpose and share the gospel.

- **Scripture Reference**: *"But you will receive power when the Holy Spirit comes on you; and you will be my witnesses in Jerusalem, and in all Judea and Samaria, and to the ends of the earth." — Acts 1:8*

Practical Steps to Walk in the Spirit

Daily Surrender:

- Begin each day by inviting the Holy Spirit to lead and guide you.
- **Prayer Example**: "Holy Spirit, I surrender my thoughts, words, and actions to You. Lead me in Your truth today."

Cultivate Spiritual Disciplines:

- Regular prayer, Bible study, worship, and fellowship are vital to staying in step with the Spirit.
- **Scripture Reference**: *"Devote yourselves to prayer, being watchful and thankful." — Colossians 4:2*

Listen and Obey:

- Be attentive to the Spirit's promptings and act in obedience, even when it's uncomfortable.
- **Illustration**: Philip obeyed the Spirit's prompting to approach the Ethiopian eunuch, resulting in a divine encounter (*Acts 8:29–35*).

Reject the Flesh:

- Actively resist sinful desires and distractions that hinder your spiritual walk.
- **Scripture Reference**: *"Put to death, therefore, whatever belongs to your earthly nature." — Colossians 3:5*

Challenges to Walking in the Spirit

Distractions and Busyness:

- A cluttered mind and schedule can drown out the voice of the Holy Spirit.
- **Solution**: Create intentional time for God each day, free from distractions.

Doubt and Fear:

- Doubting God's guidance or fearing the unknown can hinder our walk.
- **Solution**: Trust in God's promises and take steps of faith.

Spiritual Apathy:

- Growing complacent in your faith can dull your sensitivity to the Spirit.
- **Solution**: Rekindle your passion through worship, fellowship, and fasting.

Reflection Questions

1. Are you intentionally inviting the Holy Spirit to lead you daily? If not, what changes can you make to prioritize His guidance?
2. What spiritual disciplines can you strengthen to stay in step with the Spirit?
3. Are there areas in your life where the flesh is hindering your walk? How can you surrender these to God?

Empowering Declarations

- I walk in step with the Holy Spirit, guided by His wisdom and power.
- The fruit of the Spirit is evident in every area of my life.
- I overcome the desires of the flesh through the Spirit's empowerment.
- My life reflects God's glory as I walk in His Spirit daily.
- I am sensitive to the Spirit's leading and obedient to His promptings.

Final Thoughts

Walking in the Spirit is not a destination but a journey. It is a daily commitment to surrender, listen, and obey, allowing the Holy Spirit to transform and empower us for God's glory. As we align with the Spirit, we become vessels of His power, reflecting His love and purpose in a world that desperately needs Him.

> *"Since we live by the Spirit, let us keep in step with the Spirit."*
> *(Galatians 5:25)*

The Christian life is not meant to be lived in our own strength but through the power of the Holy Spirit. Walking in the Spirit involves:

- Daily surrender to His leading.
- Cultivating spiritual sensitivity through prayer and worship.
- Bearing the fruit of the Spirit (Galatians 5:22–23).

Chapter 7: The Power of the Word

"Your word is a lamp to my feet and a light for my path." **(Psalm 119:105)**

The Word of God is the foundation for understanding who we are, what we have, and what we can do in Christ. It is not merely a book; it is alive, powerful, and eternal. Many believers underestimate the transformative power of Scripture and fail to access its full potential in their lives.

The Nature of God's Word

Alive and Active:

- The Bible is not a static text but a living expression of God's will and character.
- **Scripture Reference**: *"For the word of God is alive and active. Sharper than any double-edged sword, it penetrates even to dividing soul and spirit, joints and marrow; it judges the thoughts and attitudes of the heart."* — Hebrews 4:12

Eternal and Unchanging:

- God's Word stands forever, unaffected by cultural shifts or human opinion.

- **Scripture Reference**: *"The grass withers and the flowers fall, but the word of our God endures forever."* — Isaiah 40:8

God-Breathed:

- The Scriptures are inspired by God and carry His authority.
- **Scripture Reference**: *"All Scripture is God-breathed and is useful for teaching, rebuking, correcting, and training in righteousness."* — 2 Timothy 3:16

The Functions of God's Word

Reveals God's Will and Nature:

- Through Scripture, we understand God's character, His plans, and purposes for humanity.
- **Scripture Reference**: *"Your statutes are my delight; they are my counselors."* — Psalm 119:24

Builds Faith:

- Faith comes by hearing and absorbing the Word of God.
- **Scripture Reference**: *"Consequently, faith comes from hearing the message, and the message is heard through the word about Christ."* — Romans 10:17

Transforms Minds:

- The Word renews our minds, enabling us to think and live according to God's truth.
- **Scripture Reference**: *"Do not conform to the pattern of this world, but be transformed by the renewing of your mind."* — Romans 12:2

Equips for Every Good Work:

- The Word prepares us for ministry and righteous living.
- **Scripture Reference**: *"So that the servant of God may be thoroughly equipped for every good work."* — 2 Timothy 3:17

How to Engage with the Word

Read it Daily:

- Regular reading builds familiarity and spiritual strength.
- **Practical Tip**: Establish a daily reading plan to cover both the Old and New Testaments.

Meditate on it:

- Meditation allows the Word to take root in your heart and mind.
- **Scripture Reference**: *"Keep this Book of the Law always on your lips; meditate on it day and night."* — Joshua 1:8

Study it Deeply:

- Dig into the context, meaning, and application of Scripture.
- **Practical Tip**: Use study tools like concordances, commentaries, and Bible dictionaries.

Declare it Boldly:

- Speak God's Word over your life and circumstances.
- **Scripture Reference**: *"The tongue has the power of life and death."* — Proverbs 18:21

Live it Out:

- The ultimate goal is obedience and application.
- **Scripture Reference**: *"Do not merely listen to the word, and so deceive yourselves. Do what it says." — James 1:22*

The Impact of the Word on a Believer's Life

Strengthens Against Temptation:

- Jesus used Scripture to counter the devil's temptations in the wilderness.
- **Scripture Reference**: *"Jesus answered, 'It is written: Man shall not live on bread alone, but on every word that comes from the mouth of God.'" — Matthew 4:4*

Provides Direction:

- The Word acts as a guide, showing us the path to follow.
- **Scripture Reference**: *"Your word is a lamp to my feet and a light for my path." — Psalm 119:105*

Brings Peace and Comfort:

- The promises of God's Word provide reassurance and hope.
- **Scripture Reference**: *"Great peace have those who love your law, and nothing can make them stumble." — Psalm 119:165*

Reveals our Identity:

- The Word shows us who we are in Christ and the inheritance we have as God's children.
- **Scripture Reference**: *"But you are a chosen people, a royal priesthood, a holy nation, God's special possession." — 1 Peter 2:9*

Reflection Questions

1. How often do you engage with God's Word? Are you consistent in reading, studying, and meditating on it?
2. What steps can you take to deepen your understanding of Scripture?
3. How has the Word of God transformed your life, and how can you use it to impact others?

Empowering Declarations

- God's Word is my foundation and my guide.
- I meditate on God's Word day and night, and it transforms my life.
- The promises of Scripture are active and alive in me.
- I am equipped for every good work through the power of God's Word.
- I declare victory over every challenge by speaking the truth of Scripture.

Final Thoughts

The Word of God is a priceless treasure, given to equip, guide, and transform us. By engaging with Scripture daily, meditating on its truths, and living in obedience, we can experience its full power and share its life-changing impact with others. Let us commit to making the Word central in our lives, knowing that it lights our path and reveals the heart of God.

> *"Your word is a lamp to my feet and a light for my path." (Psalm 119:105)*

The Word of God is more than a book; it is alive, powerful, and transformative. It equips us to:

- Discern truth from lies (Hebrews 4:12).
- Build faith (Romans 10:17).
- Overcome temptation (Matthew 4:4).

Chapter 8: The Book of Life and Predestination

"For those God foreknew, He also predestined to be conformed to the image of His Son." (Romans 8:29)

The concepts of the Book of Life and predestination have intrigued and, at times, confused believers for centuries. These truths, when understood in light of the new creation reality and the finished work of Christ, bring profound assurance and clarity about God's sovereign plan for humanity.

The Book of Life: God's Eternal Record

What Is the Book of Life?

- The Book of Life is referenced throughout Scripture as the record of those who belong to God and have eternal life.
- **Scripture Reference**: *"Anyone whose name was not found written in the book of life was thrown into the lake of fire."* — Revelation 20:15
- It represents God's foreknowledge and His intimate relationship with His children.

CHAPTER 8: THE BOOK OF LIFE AND PREDESTINATION

How Are Names Written in the Book?

- Names are inscribed through faith in Christ, reflecting the gift of salvation.
- **Scripture Reference**: *"Rejoice that your names are written in heaven."* — Luke 10:20
- Salvation is a gift, and our inclusion in the Book of Life is not based on works but on God's grace through faith (*Ephesians 2:8–9*).

The Security of Being Written in the Book

- Once a believer's name is written in the Book of Life, it cannot be erased.
- **Scripture Reference**: *"The one who is victorious will, like them, be dressed in white. I will never blot out the name of that person from the book of life."* — Revelation 3:5

Predestination: God's Sovereign Plan

What Is Predestination?

- Predestination refers to God's sovereign decision to call and justify those who will become His children.
- **Scripture Reference**: *"In love He predestined us for adoption to sonship through Jesus Christ, in accordance with His pleasure and will."* — Ephesians 1:4–5

God's Foreknowledge and Predestination

- God's foreknowledge does not mean He causes every event or choice but that He knows and plans for the outcome.
- **Scripture Reference**: *"For those God foreknew, He also predestined to be conformed to the image of His Son."* — Romans 8:29
- Predestination is centered on God's desire to conform us to the likeness of Christ.

Predestination and Free Will

- While God predestines, He also gives humanity free will to choose Him. These truths coexist in the mystery of His divine wisdom.
- **Illustration**: A master artist sketches a masterpiece, knowing the outcome, but the process allows for variations that still align with the vision.

Practical Applications

Rest in God's Sovereignty

- Trust that God's plan is perfect and His purposes will prevail.
- **Scripture Reference**: *"Many are the plans in a person's heart, but it is the Lord's purpose that prevails." — Proverbs 19:21*

Live Boldly in Assurance

- Let the truth of predestination and the Book of Life empower you to live without fear of rejection or failure.
- **Scripture Reference**: *"If God is for us, who can be against us?" — Romans 8:31*

Share the Gospel

- Predestination does not negate evangelism; it fuels it. We are called to share the good news, trusting God to draw people to Himself.
- **Scripture Reference**: *"How, then, can they call on the one they have not believed in? And how can they believe in the one of whom they have not heard?" — Romans 10:14*

Reflection Questions

1. How does understanding predestination impact your view of God's sovereignty and love?
2. What steps can you take to align your life with God's purpose?
3. How can the assurance of being written in the Book of Life transform the way you live?

Empowering Declarations

- My name is written in the Book of Life, and I rejoice in my salvation.
- I am predestined to be conformed to the image of Christ.
- God's plan for my life is perfect, and I trust His sovereignty.
- I live with boldness and purpose, knowing I am secure in God's love.
- I am empowered to share the gospel, trusting God to draw others to Himself.

Chapter 9: Eternal Security and Assurance of Salvation

"My sheep listen to My voice; I know them, and they follow Me. I give them eternal life, and they shall never perish; no one will snatch them out of My hand." (John 10:27-28)

The Promise of Eternal Security

Eternal security is the confident assurance that once we are saved, we are always saved. This doctrine, often called "once saved, always saved," is rooted in the finished work of Christ and the unchanging promises of God. It emphasizes the believer's safety and security in the hands of a faithful God.

Sealed by the Holy Spirit:

- The Holy Spirit is God's guarantee that we belong to Him and that He will fulfill His promises.
- **Scripture Reference**: *"When you believed, you were marked in Him with a seal, the promised Holy Spirit, who is a deposit guaranteeing our inheritance until the redemption of those who are God's possession."* — Ephesians 1:13–14

God's Faithfulness:

- Our salvation does not depend on our faithfulness but on God's. He who began a good work in us will complete it.
- **Scripture Reference**: *"Being confident of this, that He who began a good work in you will carry it on to completion until the day of Christ Jesus." — Philippians 1:6*

The Irrevocable Gift:

- Salvation is a gift, not a wage. Once given, God does not take it back.
- **Scripture Reference**: *"For God's gifts and His call are irrevocable." — Romans 11:29*

Practical Applications

Live Confidently in Christ

- Let the assurance of salvation empower you to live without fear of condemnation.

Grow in Gratitude

- Allow the certainty of God's promises to fuel your worship and commitment.

Witness Boldly

- Share the gospel with confidence, knowing that God secures those He calls.

Reflection Questions

1. How does the promise of eternal security impact your relationship with God?
2. Are there areas where fear or doubt have hindered your faith? How can you rest in God's promises?
3. How can you use the assurance of salvation to encourage others in their faith?

Chapter 10: Righteousness, Godliness, and Justification

"For He made Him who knew no sin to be sin for us, that we might become the righteousness of God in Him." (2 Corinthians 5:21)

Understanding righteousness, godliness, and justification is essential to living the victorious Christian life. These foundational truths are deeply intertwined and reveal the beauty of God's grace, the power of the cross, and the transformative reality of our identity in Christ.

Righteousness: Our Right Standing with God

The Gift of Righteousness

- Righteousness is not something we earn but a gift given freely through Christ's finished work on the cross.
- **Scripture Reference**: *"For if, by the trespass of the one man, death reigned through that one man, how much more will those who receive God's abundant provision of grace and of the gift of righteousness reign in life through the one man, Jesus Christ!"* — Romans 5:17
- This righteousness places us in perfect standing with God, regardless of our past failures.

Righteousness Through Faith

- It is by faith, not works, that we are made righteous before God.
- **Scripture Reference**: *"This righteousness is given through faith in Jesus Christ to all who believe."* — Romans 3:22

Living Out Righteousness

- While righteousness is a gift, it calls us to live in alignment with God's will and purposes.
- **Scripture Reference**: *"Little children, let no one deceive you. He who practices righteousness is righteous, just as He is righteous."* — 1 John 3:7
- Application: Reflect righteousness in your daily choices by walking in love, integrity, and holiness.

Godliness: Reflecting God's Character

What Is Godliness?

- Godliness is a life that mirrors God's character and honors Him in every thought, word, and action.
- **Scripture Reference**: *"But godliness with contentment is great gain."* — 1 Timothy 6:6

Empowered by God's Grace

- Living a godly life is made possible through the empowerment of the Holy Spirit.
- **Scripture Reference**: *"His divine power has given us everything we need for a godly life through our knowledge of Him who called us by His own glory and goodness."* — 2 Peter 1:3

Godliness in Action

- True godliness is expressed through love for others, obedience to God's Word, and a lifestyle of worship.
- **Illustration**: Godliness is like a mirror that reflects the light of Christ to the world.

Justification: Declared Righteous Before God

What Is Justification?

- Justification is a legal declaration by God, where He pronounces us righteous because of Christ's atoning sacrifice.
- **Scripture Reference**: *"Therefore, since we have been justified through faith, we have peace with God through our Lord Jesus Christ."* — Romans 5:1

The Basis of Justification

- It is solely based on God's grace and the finished work of Christ, not our own efforts.
- **Scripture Reference**: *"For all have sinned and fall short of the glory of God, and all are justified freely by His grace through the redemption that came by Christ Jesus."* — Romans 3:23–24

The Benefits of Justification

- Justification brings peace with God, access to His presence, and the assurance of eternal life.
- **Scripture Reference**: *"Who will bring any charge against those whom God has chosen? It is God who justifies."* — Romans 8:33

Living in the Light of These Truths

Rest in Righteousness

- Accept your new identity as the righteousness of God in Christ and reject feelings of guilt and unworthiness.
- **Practical Tip**: Meditate on verses about righteousness to renew your mind.

Pursue Godliness

- Cultivate a lifestyle of worship, prayer, and obedience to God's Word.
- **Application**: Identify areas in your life that need to reflect God's character more fully.

Celebrate Justification

- Live with confidence and joy, knowing that your standing before God is secure.
- **Reflection**: How does the truth of justification impact the way you approach God in prayer and worship?

Practical Applications

Daily Confessions:

- Speak these truths over your life: "I am the righteousness of God in Christ," "I live a godly life by His grace," and "I am justified by faith."

Reflect Godliness in Relationships:

- Show love, patience, and kindness in your interactions as an expression of godliness.

Share the Gospel:

- Help others understand the transformative power of righteousness, godliness, and justification.

Reflection Questions

1. How does understanding righteousness change how you see yourself and your relationship with God?
2. In what areas can you grow in godliness and reflect Christ more fully?
3. How does the assurance of justification give you confidence in your faith?

Empowering Declarations

- I am the righteousness of God in Christ Jesus.
- God's grace empowers me to live a godly life.
- I am justified by faith and have peace with God.
- My life reflects God's character and glorifies Him.
- I walk confidently, knowing that my salvation is secure in Christ.

Final Thoughts

Righteousness, godliness, and justification are not abstract theological concepts but living realities that define the believer's identity and purpose. By embracing these truths, we can live boldly for God, reflecting His glory and fulfilling His mission on earth.

Chapter 11: The Principles of Jesus and the Person of Jesus

"I am the way and the truth and the life. No one comes to the Father except through Me." (John 14:6)

To fully understand the life and teachings of Jesus, it is crucial to grasp both His principles and His person. While His principles guide us in righteous living, His person reveals the essence of God's love, power, and nature. Together, they form the foundation of a vibrant Christian life.

The Person of Jesus: The Heart of God Revealed

Jesus as God in the Flesh:

- Jesus is the exact representation of God's nature, embodying His love and holiness.
- **Scripture Reference**: *"The Son is the radiance of God's glory and the exact representation of His being, sustaining all things by His powerful word."* — Hebrews 1:3

The Humanity and Divinity of Jesus:

- Jesus fully understands our struggles because He became fully human, yet He remained fully divine.
- **Scripture Reference**: *"For we do not have a high priest who is unable to empathize with our weaknesses, but we have one who has been tempted in every way, just as we are—yet He did not sin."* — Hebrews 4:15

The Role of Jesus in Redemption:

- Jesus came to reconcile humanity to God, fulfilling the ultimate plan of salvation.
- **Scripture Reference**: *"For God was pleased to have all His fullness dwell in Him, and through Him to reconcile to Himself all things."* — Colossians 1:19–20

Relationship Over Religion:

- Jesus desires a personal relationship with us, not mere adherence to rules.
- **Illustration**: The story of Mary and Martha highlights the importance of being with Jesus over doing for Him (*Luke 10:38–42*).

The Principles of Jesus: A Blueprint for Life

Love as the Greatest Commandment:

- Jesus taught that love for God and others is the foundation of all His principles.
- **Scripture Reference**: *"'Love the Lord your God with all your heart and with all your soul and with all your mind.' This is the first and greatest commandment. And the second is like it: 'Love your neighbor as yourself.'"* — Matthew

22:37–39

Servanthood as Greatness:

- Jesus redefined greatness as serving others with humility.
- **Scripture Reference**: *"Whoever wants to become great among you must be your servant, and whoever wants to be first must be your slave—just as the Son of Man did not come to be served, but to serve."* — *Matthew 20:26–28*

Forgiveness Without Limit:

- Jesus modeled and commanded forgiveness as a non-negotiable aspect of faith.
- **Scripture Reference**: *"Then Peter came to Jesus and asked, 'Lord, how many times shall I forgive my brother or sister who sins against me? Up to seven times?' Jesus answered, 'I tell you, not seven times, but seventy-seven times.'"* — *Matthew 18:21–22*

Faith in Action:

- Jesus emphasized that faith must be demonstrated through obedience and works.
- **Scripture Reference**: *"Therefore everyone who hears these words of Mine and puts them into practice is like a wise man who built his house on the rock."* — *Matthew 7:24*

Living by Jesus' Principles Through His Person

Empowered by Relationship:

- We can only live out Jesus' principles by staying connected to Him.

- **Scripture Reference**: *"I am the vine; you are the branches. If you remain in Me and I in you, you will bear much fruit; apart from Me you can do nothing."* — *John 15:5*

Walking in His Spirit:

- The Holy Spirit enables us to embody the principles of Jesus in our daily lives.
- **Scripture Reference**: *"But the fruit of the Spirit is love, joy, peace, forbearance, kindness, goodness, faithfulness, gentleness, and self-control."* — *Galatians 5:22–23*

Reflecting His Glory:

- As we live out His principles, we reflect the person of Jesus to the world.
- **Scripture Reference**: *"Let your light shine before others, that they may see your good deeds and glorify your Father in heaven."* — *Matthew 5:16*

Practical Applications

Prioritize Time with Jesus:

- Spend time in prayer, worship, and studying His Word to deepen your relationship.
- **Reflection**: Are you prioritizing being with Jesus over doing for Him?

Practice His Principles Daily:

- Look for opportunities to love, serve, and forgive in your interactions with others.

Rely on His Spirit:

- Ask the Holy Spirit for strength and wisdom to live out Jesus' teachings.

Reflection Questions

1. How well do you know the person of Jesus? What steps can you take to deepen your relationship with Him?
2. Which principle of Jesus do you find most challenging to live out? Why?
3. How can you reflect the person and principles of Jesus to those around you this week?

Empowering Declarations

- Jesus is my Lord and Savior; I live in relationship with Him daily.
- I am empowered by the Holy Spirit to live out Jesus' principles.
- My life reflects the love, grace, and truth of Jesus to the world.
- I walk in forgiveness, faith, and servanthood, embodying the teachings of Christ.
- I am a light in the world, glorifying my Father in heaven.

Final Thoughts

The principles of Jesus and the person of Jesus cannot be separated. His teachings guide us, but His presence empowers us. By embracing both, we can live a life that honors God, impacts others, and fulfills our purpose in Christ.

Chapter 12: The Holy Spirit and the Church

"But you will receive power when the Holy Spirit comes on you; and you will be my witnesses in Jerusalem, and in all Judea and Samaria, and to the ends of the earth." (*Acts 1:8*)

The Holy Spirit is the heartbeat of the Church. From the early days of Pentecost to the present, the Church's power, unity, and mission have always depended on the Holy Spirit. Yet, many believers do not fully understand His role in their personal lives or in the corporate life of the Church.

Who Is the Holy Spirit?

The Holy Spirit is the third person of the Trinity, co-equal with God the Father and God the Son. He is not a force or an abstract power but a divine person who has emotions, will, and intellect.

- **God's Presence**: The Holy Spirit is the presence of God dwelling among us and within us (**1 Corinthians 3:16**).
- **The Comforter**: Jesus referred to Him as the Comforter or Advocate who would come to guide and support believers (**John 14:26**).
- **The Spirit of Truth**: He leads us into all truth, revealing the mysteries of God and His Word (**John 16:13**).

His Role in Our Lives

The Holy Spirit plays an integral role in the life of every believer:

- **Conviction of Sin**: He convicts the world of sin, righteousness, and judgment, leading people to repentance (**John 16:8**).
- **Regeneration**: He brings new life to believers, making them spiritually alive in Christ (**Titus 3:5**).
- **Empowerment**: The Spirit empowers believers to live victoriously and boldly share the gospel (**Acts 1:8**).
- **Sanctification**: He works within us to make us more like Christ, producing the fruit of the Spirit in our lives (**Galatians 5:22–23**).
- **Intercession**: The Holy Spirit intercedes for us in prayer, helping us when we do not know what to pray (**Romans 8:26–27**).

The Role of the Holy Spirit in the Church

- **Empowering the Church**: The Holy Spirit empowers believers to fulfill the Great Commission. He provides the boldness and gifts needed to share the gospel effectively (**Acts 4:31, 1 Corinthians 12:7–11**).
- **Building Unity**: The Holy Spirit unites the Church as one body, regardless of cultural, ethnic, or social differences. This unity reflects the love of Christ to the world (**Ephesians 4:3–6**).
- **Equipping with Spiritual Gifts**: The Spirit equips believers with gifts for service, such as teaching, prophecy, healing, and encouragement, to build up the Church (**1 Corinthians 12:4–11, Romans 12:6–8**).
- **Guiding and Leading**: The Spirit provides wisdom and direction to both individuals and the Church as a whole. He reveals God's will and ensures the Church stays aligned with God's purposes (**John 16:13, Acts 13:2**).

The Day of Pentecost: A Model for the Church

The events of Pentecost (Acts 2) illustrate the transformative power of the Holy Spirit in the Church:

- **Unity in Prayer**: The early believers gathered in unity and prayer, creating an atmosphere for the Spirit to move.
- **Empowerment for Witness**: The Holy Spirit enabled them to speak in tongues and share the gospel with people from diverse backgrounds.
- **A Global Mission**: Pentecost marked the beginning of the Church's mission to reach the world with the message of Christ.

The Holy Spirit's Presence in Worship

- **True Worship**: The Holy Spirit leads believers into authentic worship that glorifies God in spirit and truth (**John 4:24**).
- **Manifestation of God's Presence**: During worship, the Spirit often manifests God's presence, bringing comfort, conviction, healing, and joy (**2 Corinthians 3:17, Psalm 16:11**).

Hindrances to the Holy Spirit's Work in the Church

- **Quenching the Spirit**: When believers ignore the Spirit's leading or fail to exercise faith, they limit His work (**1 Thessalonians 5:19**).
- **Division and Strife**: Disunity among believers grieves the Spirit and hinders His work (**Ephesians 4:30–31**).
- **Neglecting Spiritual Gifts**: When the Church neglects or misuses spiritual gifts, it fails to operate in the fullness of the Spirit's power.

CHAPTER 12: THE HOLY SPIRIT AND THE CHURCH

Practical Applications

- **Pray for a Fresh Outpouring**: Regularly seek the infilling of the Holy Spirit for personal and corporate renewal (**Ephesians 5:18**).
- **Cultivate Unity**: Actively work to preserve unity in the Church by fostering love, forgiveness, and understanding (**Colossians 3:13–14**).
- **Exercise Spiritual Gifts**: Discover and use your spiritual gifts to serve others and build up the Church.
- **Follow the Spirit's Leading**: Stay sensitive to the Spirit's guidance in your decisions, relationships, and ministry.

Reflection Questions

1. How has the Holy Spirit empowered you personally in your walk with Christ?
2. What steps can you take to cultivate unity in your local church?
3. Are you fully using the spiritual gifts God has given you? If not, what can you do to begin?
4. How can your church rely more on the Holy Spirit for guidance and power?

By embracing the role of the Holy Spirit in the Church, we can experience a greater measure of God's power, unity, and presence. The Spirit is not an optional part of the Christian life; He is essential to the mission and vitality of the Church.

Chapter 13: Loving Without Offense

"**A new command I give you: Love one another. As I have loved you, so you must love one another. By this everyone will know that you are my disciples, if you love one another.**" (*John 13:34–35*)

Loving without offense is one of the greatest challenges and highest callings in the life of a believer. In a world full of misunderstandings, hurts, and division, the ability to love unconditionally and without taking offense sets us apart as followers of Christ. Yet, this kind of love is often overlooked or misunderstood in the Church.

Understanding Love Without Offense

- **The Love of Christ as Our Example**: Jesus exemplified love without offense, even in the face of betrayal, rejection, and persecution. He chose forgiveness over resentment and compassion over judgment (**Luke 23:34**).
- **Love as a Choice, Not a Feeling**: Loving without offense requires intentionality. It is a decision to reflect God's character rather than respond from our emotions (**1 Corinthians 13:4–7**).
- **Guarding Your Heart**: Taking offense often stems from unresolved hurts or pride. The Bible instructs us to guard our hearts and respond with grace (**Proverbs 4:23, Colossians 4:6**).

Why Loving Without Offense Matters

- **It Reflects God's Nature**: God's love is unconditional and unchanging. As His children, we are called to love in the same way (**1 John 4:19**).
- **It Promotes Unity**: Offense divides relationships and weakens the body of Christ. Choosing love fosters unity and strength in the Church (**Ephesians 4:3**).
- **It Is a Witness to the World**: Our ability to love without offense demonstrates the transformative power of the gospel (**John 13:35**).

Overcoming the Temptation to Take Offense

- **Practice Forgiveness**: Forgiveness is the foundation of love without offense. Jesus taught us to forgive not just once, but repeatedly (**Matthew 18:21–22**).
- **Assume the Best**: Rather than jumping to conclusions or harboring bitterness, choose to believe the best about others' intentions (**Philippians 4:8**).
- **Rely on the Holy Spirit**: The Holy Spirit empowers us to love and respond with grace, even in difficult situations (**Romans 5:5**).

Practical Steps to Love Without Offense

1. **Pause Before Reacting**: When hurt or offended, take a moment to pray and seek God's wisdom before responding (**James 1:19–20**).
2. **Speak the Truth in Love**: Address misunderstandings or conflicts with gentleness and respect, aiming for reconciliation rather than confrontation (**Ephesians 4:15**).
3. **Pray for Those Who Hurt You**: Praying for others softens your heart and aligns your perspective with God's (**Matthew 5:44**).
4. **Embrace Humility**: Recognize that we all fall short and need grace. Humility opens the door for healing and reconciliation (**Philippians 2:3–4**).

Reflection Questions

1. Are there areas in your life where you are holding onto offense? How can you release it and choose forgiveness?
2. How does Christ's example of love challenge you to respond differently in difficult relationships?
3. What practical steps can you take to guard your heart and love others unconditionally?

Empowering Declarations

- I choose to love as Christ loves me, without holding onto offense.
- I forgive freely and trust God to heal my heart and relationships.
- I reflect God's unconditional love in every interaction.
- My love promotes unity and strengthens the body of Christ.
- I rely on the Holy Spirit to empower me to love beyond my natural ability.

Loving without offense is not just a command—it is a transformative way of life that sets believers apart and reveals the heart of God to a hurting world. By choosing love over offense, we become vessels of His grace, ambassadors of His kingdom, and reflections of His glory.

Conclusion: Walking Boldly in Truth

As we come to the end of this journey, let us reflect on the truths we have uncovered and the transformative power they hold for every believer. The revelation of our identity in Christ, the finished work of the cross, the empowerment of the Holy Spirit, and the call to walk in love without offense are not just theological concepts—they are the foundations of a victorious Christian life.

God has equipped you with everything you need to live boldly and confidently in His love and purpose. You are a new creation, empowered by His grace, walking in His authority, and guided by His Spirit. These truths are not reserved for a select few but are freely available to all who believe.

As you step forward, remember that the journey of faith is one of continual growth and discovery. Let the Holy Spirit lead you deeper into the knowledge of God's love, His Word, and His will for your life. Embrace the freedom and victory that come from fully trusting in His promises and live as a beacon of His light to those around you.

The truths shared in this book are an invitation to experience the fullness of God's plan for your life. They are a call to walk in unity, love, and purpose, reflecting the glory of Christ in everything you do. May you go forth with courage, faith, and the unwavering knowledge that you are deeply loved, fully accepted, and divinely empowered.

Thank you for embarking on this journey. May the truths you have discovered here transform your life and inspire you to share the gospel of Christ with boldness and love.

About the Author

Ese Duke is an anointed teacher, author, and minister of the gospel with a divine mandate rooted in **Isaiah 61:1-2**: to proclaim the good news, bring freedom to the oppressed, and reveal the transformative power of God's Spirit. As the founder of **Spirit Temple University**, headquartered in Arizona, USA, and the president of **Spiritual Father Apostolic Covering**, Ese Duke has devoted his life to empowering believers around the world to live in the fullness of their God-given identity.

Ese Duke is also the author of several impactful books, including:

The Presence of God: A Supernatural Experience (ISBN: 978-1-6657-1309-2)

The Anointing: The Supernatural Power of God (ISBN: 978-1-4808-7031-4)

The Mind: The Control Center of Your Life (ISBN: 978-1-6657—5581-8)

These books, available in bookstores and on Amazon, have inspired countless readers by revealing deep insights into God's power, presence, and purpose.

As a leader and pastor at **Spirit Temple Bible Church**, Ese Duke ministers to a global congregation with teachings that emphasize the believer's authority in Christ, the empowerment of the Holy Spirit, and the life-changing truths of God's Word. His ability to articulate complex spiritual concepts in a simple and practical way has made him a sought-after speaker and mentor.

Beyond his ministry, Ese Duke is a loving husband to **Gladys Duke** and a devoted father to their children. His family remains his constant source of support and inspiration as he fulfills God's calling to impact lives for His glory.

With a passion for teaching and a heart for equipping the Church, Ese Duke continues to inspire believers to embrace their identity in Christ, walk in divine purpose, and experience the supernatural power of God in their daily lives.

You can connect with me on:
- https://esedukeministry.org
- https://www.facebook.com/esedukemiracleministry

Also by Ese Duke

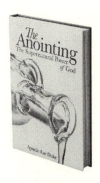

The Anointing: The Supernatural Power of God

In *The Anointing*, author Apostle Ese Duke offers a reverential look at the anointing of the Holy Spirit, the supernatural power of God that gives believers the ability to fulfill their God-given purpose. Apostle Ese Duke discusses:

What the anointing is

How to prepare to receive the anointing

The levels and dimensions of the anointing

The laws operating the anointing

The difference between the anointing within and the anointing upon

How the anointing functions and grows

How to release the anointing

How to keep the anointing flowing and many more impactful, life-changing teachings

The Anointing presents a look at God's power working in an ordinary man to bring about the supernatural in the lives and affairs of men.

The Presence of God: A Supernatural Experience

In *The Presence of God,* author Ese Duke shows you how to engage the supernatural in your humanity and thereby walk and manifest God's presence wherever you are. This guide takes you to a place of supernatural living beyond your imagination, a reality that God desires all of us to experience, yet only a few have and do.

When you understand how to live out of the presence of God, everything becomes easy. In *The Presence of God,* you will learn:

What God's presence is

How to live out of His presence, making the realities of the presence of God become manifested in your everyday life

How to manifest God's presence, even on demand

How to engage the spirit realm and get results.

Get ready to move to the highest dimension of the supernatural in your life.

Pick up a copy today at your favorite bookstore!

The Mind: The Control Center of Your Life

Do you want to cultivate a winning mindset? Do you want to succeed in life? Have you entertained troubling thoughts that won't go away? Does your mind wander uncontrollably? If you falter in the faculty called the mind, you will fail in life, regardless of how fervently you pray.

In *The Mind*, author Ese Duke shows you how to manage your imagination by training your mind to align with the word of God. He teaches you how to cleanse your imagination so those thoughts won't overtake you. He also shows you steps to take to regain control of your mind.

Duke shares how the mind is an indispensable asset given to you by God to process information and relate with the spirit. If you can understand the workings of the mind, you can better comprehend and succeed in life. The mind is the control center of our lives, and *The Mind* offers a study to help you become a master of self and life.

Made in the USA
Columbia, SC
05 February 2025